WATER

Troll Associates

WATER

by Rae Bains

Illustrated by T.R. Garcia

Troll Associates

Library of Congress Cataloging in Publication Data

Bains, Rae.
    Water.

    Summary: Explains the importance of water to our bodies,
our lives, all other living creatures, and the earth it-
self, and discusses evaporation and rainfall.
    1. Water—Juvenile literature. [1. Water] I. García,
T. R., ill. II. Title.
GV662.3.B35   1985   546′.22   84-2718
ISBN 0-8167-0194-6 (lib. bdg.)
ISBN 0-8167-0195-4 (pbk.)

Water is everywhere. It is at the top of the highest mountains. If you dig a hole deep into the ground, you'll reach water. Water comes out of the sky as rain and snow. It drifts around us as fog. We swim in it, drink it, and brush our teeth with it.

Water is an important part of our lives all the time. It is also an important part of ourselves. For every ten pounds you weigh, seven pounds is water. There is water in your skin, your blood, your bones—in every cell of your body.

Most of the Earth itself is covered by water. It flows in brooks, streams, and rivers. It bubbles over stones and tumbles down cliffs in mighty falls. Ocean waves surge and hammer against sandy shores and rocky coastlines.

Huge masses of ice, called *glaciers*, press into the Earth as they move slowly, cutting deep hollows in one place and raising mountains in another. In all of its forms, everywhere in the world, water is always changing and reshaping our planet.

Water is needed by every living thing on Earth. Plants take in water from the soil through their roots, and from the air through their leaves. They use the water, along with sunlight, to grow and to produce flowers and fruit.

Animals need water to stay alive. And people also must have water to survive. If you eat no food for about three days, you will be very hungry, but in no real danger. But three days without water can be very dangerous. Every cell in a person's body *must* have water in it and around it all the time.

The water in our bodies is in a form called a liquid. A lake is liquid water, too. So are raindrops, ocean waves, and what pours from a garden hose and a fire hydrant. Liquid water flows, splashes, drips, and bubbles.

For water to stay in liquid form, it must not be too hot or too cold. When liquid water is heated enough, it changes into another form called a gas. The change is called *evaporation*, and the gas is called *water vapor*.

There is water vapor in the air all the time, even though we usually cannot see it. But there are times when it's easy to see. A fog that swirls close to the ground is water vapor. The white puffs that you breathe out on a cold day are water vapor, too.

Have you ever seen water change from a liquid to a gas? You probably have, right in your own kitchen. When a pot of water is placed over a flame, the water grows warmer and warmer. In a while, wispy threads of mist rise off the top of the water. This rising mist is called steam.

Steam is hot water vapor. Liquid water begins to turn into steam when it reaches a very high temperature called the boiling point. If water continues to boil, it will soon disappear. Where has all the water gone? Into the air, as a gas.

You have also seen water change from a gas to a liquid. When you breathe on a mirror, you see a small cloud on it. Touch it and you'll find it is wet. The wetness is water vapor that was in the air you breathed out. When it touched the cool mirror, the vapor changed from a gas to a liquid. This change is called *condensation*.

Any time air touches a cold surface, the water vapor in the air condenses into a liquid.

When liquid water is cooled enough, it reaches the very low temperature called the freezing point. Then it changes into another form called a solid. This change is known as freezing, and the solid form of water is known as ice. You can see ice in the freezer section of a refrigerator. And every time you look at snow, you are seeing millions of ice crystals.

In most of the world, we see snow and ice only in the winter. But at the North and South Poles, there is ice all year round. That is because the temperature at the poles is always below the freezing point.

Imagine you are able to take a trip with a drop of liquid water. When the trip starts, the drop of water is part of a lake. One day bright sunshine warms the lake. Soon the drop of water gets warm enough to turn into water vapor.

The vapor rises through the air and becomes part of a cloud. The cloud is carried along by the winds. As it sweeps through the sky, the cloud picks up more and more water vapor. At last, when the cloud is heavy with water, rain begins to fall.

Our drop of water is part of this rain. It lands on the soil next to a peach tree. The

drop sinks deep into the soil, where it is taken in by a root of the tree.

The tree uses the water to help it grow fruit. When you eat a peach from this tree, you take in that drop of water. Now it is a part of you.

The next day you're running and playing in the sunshine. You feel very warm and begin to perspire. One of the drops of water on your perspiring face is the one we are following.

Soon the sunshine turns the drop into water vapor again. Once more it rises into the air, and once more the wind carries it away.

The same drop of water can go through many changes, and it can travel to every corner of the world. Each move and each change a drop of water goes through is part of the water cycle.

The word *cycle* means "circle." Just as a bicycle wheel goes around and around in a circle, so does water. It goes up from the land to the sky, down to the ocean, up to the sky again, down to a mountain, and so on, in an endless circle. This cycle has been going on since the Earth was first covered with water.

If there were no water vapor in the sky, there would be no rain or snow. Of course, wet weather can keep us indoors, but we need it!

Just think of what happens if there isn't much rain or snow for a year or more. The land grows dry and plants die. Topsoil turns to dust and wind blows it away. We call this condition a drought. A drought that lasts a long time is a terrible thing!

At times it rains or snows too much, and that can be just as terrible. When there is more water than the rivers, reservoirs, and ground can hold, we have floods. Swollen rivers overflow their banks, washing away topsoil and drowning farm crops and trees.

Flood waters damage our homes and highways, and take the lives of people and animals. Water, a great friend of people, can also be a horrible enemy!

What is this powerful, necessary thing called water? In all of its forms—gas, liquid, and solid—water is a combination of two chemical elements. These elements are hydrogen and oxygen.

When one atom of oxygen combines with two atoms of hydrogen, they lock together very tightly. The tightly locked combination is called a molecule of water.

We cannot see a molecule of water because it is so small. It is too small for us to see even through the strongest microscope. Only when many, many of these molecules are joined together can we see them as one tiny drop of water.

Water molecules are exactly the same in the water from your kitchen faucet and in ocean water. Then why do they taste so different? Because ocean water isn't just water. It also has salt in it.

Pure water, all by itself, is tasteless. But it can carry the taste of anything dissolved in it, such as sugar, salt, or chemicals from the ground.

The water that is stored in reservoirs for us to use must be cleaned so that it is safe to drink. Dirty, polluted water can cause disease. So all germs and impurities are removed before the water enters our homes.

Farmers use water to grow the food we eat. They irrigate, or water their crops, to increase the harvest. Industry uses water, too. Water cleans and cools machines. It is needed in the manufacture of glass, steel, plastics, chemicals, medicines, and thousands of other products.

Water power drives huge machines that send electricity to our homes and businesses.

We also use water for travel and shipping. Ships carry people and products from place to place over the world's rivers, lakes, and oceans.

Since ancient times, people have said that fresh water is worth more than gold, silver, and diamonds. It was true long ago, and it is true today. All the living things on Earth could survive without jewels and precious metals. But without water, the world we know would soon disappear.